THIS IS ME! 2022

IN MY WORDS

Edited By Roseanna Caswell

First published in Great Britain in 2022 by:

YoungWriters® Est. 1991

Young Writers
Remus House
Coltsfoot Drive
Peterborough
PE2 9BF
Telephone: 01733 890066
Website: www.youngwriters.co.uk

All Rights Reserved
Book Design by Ashley Janson
© Copyright Contributors 2022
Softback ISBN 978-1-80459-048-5

Printed and bound in the UK by BookPrintingUK
Website: www.bookprintinguk.com
YB0509R

FOREWORD

For Young Writers' latest competition This Is Me, we asked primary school pupils to look inside themselves, to think about what makes them unique, and then write a poem about it! They rose to the challenge magnificently and the result is this fantastic collection of poems in a variety of poetic styles.

Here at Young Writers our aim is to encourage creativity in children and to inspire a love of the written word, so it's great to get such an amazing response, with some absolutely fantastic poems. It's important for children to focus on and celebrate themselves and this competition allowed them to write freely and honestly, celebrating what makes them great, expressing their hopes and fears, or simply writing about their favourite things. This Is Me gave them the power of words. The result is a collection of inspirational and moving poems that also showcase their creativity and writing ability.

I'd like to congratulate all the young poets in this anthology, I hope this inspires them to continue with their creative writing.

CONTENTS

Barnhill Primary School, Broughty Ferry

Isaac Dunn	1
Carmen Dempster	2
Lucy Coull	3

Corsham Regis Primary Academy, Corsham

Ashlee Graham (11)	4
Mya C	6
Jett C	7
Eva Booth (10)	8

Easington Colliery Primary School, Easington Colliery

Shay Storey-Hogg (11)	9
Lily Mika (11)	10
Jaiden (11)	12
Ava	14
India (11)	16
Ella Wood (11)	18
Mia Robinson (10)	20
Megan O'Neil (10)	22
Genevieve Sullivan (11)	23
Connor Morrow (10)	24
Noah B (11)	26
Bobby Chilton (10)	28
Mason Fox (10)	30
Phoebe Harrison (11)	31
Daniel W (10)	32
Lacey Jane Scott (11)	34
Kayla Fergus (10)	35
Finlay (10)	36
Jayden D (10)	37
Layton (11)	38
Sophie D (11)	39
Lilly Mae Robinson (11)	40
Lilly-May Pearson (11)	41
Evie Wilson (10)	42
Declan B (11)	43
Logan A (10)	44
Hollie (10)	45
Aidan C (10)	46
Stewart (11)	47
Ruby (11)	48
Mason W (11)	49
Tyler Gallagher (10)	50
Olivia K (11)	51
Riley Foster (11)	52
Aaliyah Brown (10)	53
Rhys M (11)	54
Emmi (11)	55
Callum Fishburn (11)	56
Declan C (11)	57
Krystal Ward (10)	58
Olivia Cockfield (10)	59
Jaxon (10)	60
Josh C (11)	61
Bruce Langlands (10)	62
Kenzie B (11)	63
Ella R (11)	64
Kayla C (11)	65
Jake Oliver (10)	66
Lily May (10)	67
Kai (11)	68
Nora (10)	69
Jenson Price (11)	70
Amii Louise W (10)	71

Ryan Pine (10)	72
Layla E (10)	73

Loretto Junior School, Musselburgh

Evangelos Pappas (10)	74
Rose Adams (10)	77
Ava Shanks (10)	78
Hamish Fergusson (10)	80
Charlotte Gordon (10)	82
Lucas Teague (10)	84
Murray Allister (11)	86
Bracken Kirk (11)	88
Ewan Kay (11)	89
Megan Hill (10)	90
Kitty Strang-Steel (11)	92
Francesca Jones (10)	93

Our Lady of Perpetual Succour Primary School, Widnes

Lilly Varley (9)	94
George Connor (10)	95
Ewan Ainsworth (10)	96
Clayton Tomlinson (10)	97
Bobby Abbott (9)	98
Louie Gore (9)	99
Brooke Burrows (9)	100
Lucas Campbell (10)	101
Daisy Roche (9)	102
Charlie Capewell (10)	103
Ethan G (9)	104
Jasmine Winders (10)	105
Jack Butler (10)	106
Toby Sinclair (9)	107
Erin Tyrer (10)	108
Erin Dourley (10)	109
Lexie Dwyer (10)	110
Sam Turpin (10)	111
Niamh Collins (9)	112
Billy Purcell (9)	113
Ethan Fox (10)	114
Charlie Edwards (9)	115

Savannah Fitzpatrick (9)	116
James Shields (10)	117
Bella Sheridan (9)	118

St Aidan's Catholic Primary Academy, Ilford

Franco Anthony Alcala (9)	119
Sithi Ghosh (14)	120
Sophia Russo (8)	122
Asaad	123
Evelina Niculae (8)	124
Lucca Pavanello (9)	125

St Mary's Catholic Primary School, Tilbury

Morgan Agu (10)	126
Dorinda Ametefe (8)	128
Marrianne Azaka-Ekpeti (10)	130
Ifechukwude Emmanuel Nwaokolo (10)	132
Harry Morris (11)	134
Erin Asemota	136
Titoluwanimi Tunde-Oke (10)	138
Michelle Dongmo (9)	139
Neytiri Sinclair (9)	140
Theresa Iloene (8)	142
Precious Ogunsola (9)	144
Rebecca Bamidele	145
Abigail Blake (11)	146
Mara Calin (8)	148
Summer O'Brien (11)	149
Samantha Falusi	150
Kengah Happi (10)	151
Giselle Rowland (10)	152
Hannah Joan Blake (11)	153
Godadom Boafo (7)	154
Ayodamola Falayi (10)	155
Imisioluwa Kabiawu (9)	156
Samuel Oboite (9)	157
Nabeelah Jokosanya (8)	158
Adedamola Adeyemo (8)	159
Victoria-Florence Uzomah (8)	160

Temiloluwa Owoeye (9)	161
Seun Oladokun	162
Sola Oladokun	163

Tweedmouth Community Middle School, Spittal

William Forster (10)	164
Casey Mole (11)	166
Dylan McCleary (11)	168
Faye Robertson (11)	169
Nico McEwen (11)	170
Bethan Doonan (10)	171
Romy Wilson (10)	172
Seren Bird (10)	173
Poppy Mcdonald (11)	174
Caleb Punton (10)	176
Lexi Burgon (10)	178
Louis Outterson (11)	179
Damon Dobson (11)	180
Michalina Zielinska (11)	181
Charlotte Richardson (11)	182
Marion Mavin (10)	183
Lennox Hannan (10)	184
Luke Meakin (10)	186
Charlie Tait (10)	187
Layton Ellis (11)	188
Nicole Johnson (11)	189
Lars Manteuffel (10)	190
John Mcenaney (10)	191
Alice Brown (10)	192
Aidan Johnstone (11)	193
Ruby Lambert (10)	194
Yasmeen Eldessouky (10)	195
Camila Martins (10)	196
Theo Forrest (10)	197
Dexter Hogarth-Johnson (11)	198
Rhys Morrison (10)	199
Blake Scott (10)	200
Mason Mitchell (11)	201
Ryan Young (10)	202
Chloe Renner (11)	203
Jack Wardhaugh (11)	204
Layla Brown (11)	205
Maisie Wright (11)	206
Shaun Murray	207
Ruby Buchan (11)	208
Robyn Mason (11)	209
James Gibson (10)	210
Noel Howe (10)	211
Jack Hoskins (10)	212
Mason Graham (11)	213
Taylor Burgon (11)	214
Isabelle Turley (11)	215
Toby Trotter (10)	216
Mackenzie Purvis (10)	217
Trulli Hogg (10)	218
Luis Palmero-Iglesias (11)	219
Laila-May Blackie (10)	220
Dylan Flatman (10)	221
Leon Powling (11)	222
Harry Curle (10)	223
Finley Bartell (11)	224
Savannah Brown (10)	225
Lilly Tait (10)	226
Jake Fleming (11)	227
Alyssa Tucker (10)	228
Alexia Catterall (11)	229

THE POEMS

This Is Me

My name is Isaac and I'm eleven
My favourite number is seven
My favourite footballer is Ronaldo, siuuuu
Messi is as good as gold though
FIFA is the game I play most
I'm pretty good, not to boast
I play my Xbox as much as I can
PlayStation is like its little brother, I'm not a fan
My friends call me the funny guy
Sometimes they laugh so much it's like they're going to die
Winter and the cold is my favourite season
Even though we are all freezing
On YouTube, I watch Pieface
The FIFA sub count is like an Olympic race.

Isaac Dunn
Barnhill Primary School, Broughty Ferry

My Hero

When you smile, the world is cast in light
When you stop, we float into a deadly night
Your eyes are like a strong oak tree
I don't think anybody is luckier than me!
Your personality is strong, no day is ever grey
I even love our content home by the silky River Tay
So, Mother, I hope you see
You are a real hero to me
You always believe in my dreams
You're a star, surrounded by beams!

Carmen Dempster
Barnhill Primary School, Broughty Ferry

Nature And Me

Sometimes I wonder
How the world creates thunder

My favourite climbing tree
Is what best describes me

It just stands there all calm
That tree is an important piece of who I am

I like to sit in the cold dark night
Sometimes it just sets me right

My ideas fall like lilac leaves
But to plant more nature we must roll up our sleeves.

Lucy Coull
Barnhill Primary School, Broughty Ferry

Earth

Earth is big and round
Too round for me to see
A plastic bottle is all I have found
That is home to a lonely bee

Earth is big and round
Rough and rocky too
It makes me feel tiny
In my bean can, that's shiny

Earth is big and round
With its sunsets and views
Humans use the planet
As a bin that's free to use

Earth is big and round
Its gravity is strong
But the atmosphere is piercing
And its time left isn't very long

Earth is big and round
We need to stop littering
So enjoy the fresh air
And enjoy picking pears.

Ashlee Graham (11)
Corsham Regis Primary Academy, Corsham

Dictionary

When I open my dictionary
I get words like ping, pong and bang
And ones like ting, tong and tang
My dictionary helps me find words and meaning
And it makes my book look beaming
My dictionary doesn't find words that rhyme
But it helps me spell words like time and mime
My dictionary has a variety of words
It's so useful it can be used by birds
Yes, it can be struck by lightning
Yes, it's frightening
But my dictionary is small and bold
And is immune to the cold.

Mya C
Corsham Regis Primary Academy, Corsham

January
Inspired by 'The Raven' by Edgar Allen Poe

'Twas upon a midnight dreary
As I pondered weak and weary
I heard a tapping at my door
And the crows that crow nevermore
Distinctly I remember 'twas upon the bleak December
As trapped in dark, the light came forth
Vividly I remember January lasts forever
Crushed to dust and heart that aches
Through all and all and all that aches
Heart of void wish I couldn't feel
And heartache feels almost unreal.

Jett C
Corsham Regis Primary Academy, Corsham

One Kind Word

One kind thing
Can change someone's life from sad to happy
That's why you should be kind
It only takes
One kind word
One kind thing
One kind action
One kind hug
To make glow
If you make someone glow you're a lovely person
And it can change someone's life forever
Just be caring and kind.

Eva Booth (10)
Corsham Regis Primary Academy, Corsham

This Is Me

Hello, I'm Shay
I am here to speak to you today
About me this is me
I'm smart, I'm kind
Got a really fast mind
Most people call me annoying but I don't care
To be honest, I don't think that's fair
All I am is myself, I like it that way
If you don't like it you can go away
If you got to know me you would know I'm kind
All I try to do is make you feel fine
Sometimes that doesn't work but I try my best
I am sporty also you can come and play
But just saying this, don't ruin the game
I like to sing and that's really true
Sometimes I sing with someone
Who I would give a 5-star review
I like basketball and football
And a little bit of dodgeball too
But the one thing that's true is
This is me.

Shay Storey-Hogg (11)
Easington Colliery Primary School, Easington Colliery

This Is Me

My name is Lily,
Like the flower lily.
I can be more interesting than you may think,
I honestly want to go to an ice rink.
I dislike my name,
I'm not a lass or a dame.
I'm non-binary and happy to be,
And would rather have names such as these:
Wilbur, Zero, Six, Blank or Dusk.

As a fun fact for you, which I've learned,
Dusk means choke or twilight in Lithuanian.
I have a vast varied amount of knowledge,
To be fair, I can't decide whether to go to college.
The best decision might be to do so,
I prefer the rain to fog and snow.

My knowledge varies greatly,
I like staying up more lately.
I love ramen, lunch and brunch,
And I love hearing beneath my feet the snow crunch.

I can be very mysterious like a flower blooming,
Or a silent flower snoozing.

I might be quiet,
I like to spend time alone and not in a riot.
Lots of times I can zone out like a clone,
If I'm excited I can go on like a drone.

I'm an introvert,
And an atheist but not a convert.
Although I always wonder,
And I can really sometimes ponder,
What do people really live for?
Some may say for love or 'the one',
But I'm not sure if that's a pro or a con.
It could be worthwhile though if you work hard for it,
It can be well deserved so I hope those who are lucky find it.

Lily Mika (11)
Easington Colliery Primary School, Easington Colliery

This Is Me

To make me, you will need:
Two bathtubs of kindness
One litre of strong
Two ounces of purple
Five hundred millilitres of protective
A sprinkle of jokes
One litre of football
Three litres of happiness
One drop of sadness
Five pots of family
Ten cups of friends
Five hundred millilitres of movies
One bathtub of braveness
One teaspoon of rudeness

You can start with two bathtubs of kindness
Add five hundred millilitres of strong to each so it makes 1000 litres
Then add one ounce of purple to each
Add five hundred millilitres of protective to one bathtub
Add a sprinkle of jokes to the second bathtub

Add one full litre of football to one bathtub
Then add three litres of happiness
Add one drop of sadness
Add five pans of family
Then ten cups of friends
Five hundred millilitres movies
One bathtub of braveness
One teaspoon of rudeness
Then stir, stir, stir!

Jaiden (11)
Easington Colliery Primary School, Easington Colliery

How To Make Me!

To make me, you will need...
60g of creativity
5lb of happiness
A jar of insecurities
A pot full of silliness
A squeeze of curiosity
1kg of worries
A dash of sports
850ml of intelligence
A gallon of messiness
Ten cups of love
Four pounds of humour
And finally, a drizzle of craziness!

Start with the creativity in a pan
Slowly add in insecurities then turn on the stove at 70 degrees for five mins
Separately, put some sports, intelligence, love and messiness in a bowl
After the main mix has been left for five minutes
You must add the separate mixture in
Now lay in the worries, which should be followed by happiness and a squeeze of curiosity

Let it sit for twenty minutes
And for the last touch, add a drizzle of craziness!

Now you have me!
What do I need to make you?

Ava
Easington Colliery Primary School, Easington Colliery

This Makes Me, Me

Pasta is my favourite food
It makes me happy and brightens my mood
I'm really really tall
And my confidence is not small
I like to play cricket
But barely hit the wickets
This makes me, me

Blonde hair, hazel eyes
I like to take pictures of pretty skies
My favourite colour is green
But not the pencil colour green
I'm tidy but messy
I'm not a fan of dressing dressy
This is what makes me, me

I really want to slay
Want to Beyoncé like Beyoncé
I'm quite sporty
And sometimes naughty
Kind of insecure

But my family makes me feel secure
This is what makes me, me

I want to model for Versace
And buy from Burberry
I treasure my friends
Love them till the end
People know me as the youngest
Three sisters if you count the oldest,
This is what makes me, me.

India (11)
Easington Colliery Primary School, Easington Colliery

More Than You Think

You may think I'm boring
You may think I'm bland
But this is what a lot of people don't
quite understand

I'm not just a 'know-it-all'
With chocolate hair and eyes
There is more about me hidden not so deep inside

I can be good fun
I can have a laugh
I can have great fun with friends wherever I am at

I love eating pizza
Popcorn and savoury too
Too many take for granted our huge Earth's
lovely food

Athletic is my middle name
So, I always run about
Netball, tennis, and basketball I adore without
a doubt

I climb up mammoth mountains
Just to reach a single star
My resilience can make it shine for many miles far

So, you might think I'm weird
And that I'm just obscene
But I am the best type of me the world has
ever seen.

Ella Wood (11)
Easington Colliery Primary School, Easington Colliery

This Is Me

The ingredients to make a Mia muffin...

You will need:
1/4 cup of kindness
A dash of pink and blue
A jar of loyalty
A teaspoon of rudeness
A pinch of spiciness
A bowl of sassiness
A sprinkle of me being respectful
A spoonful of sloths, fish and lamas
A little bit of a cheetah
A big spoonful of goofiness
1,000 jars of loudness
Lots of confidence

Now what to do:
Stir in 1/4 cup of kindness
Then a dash of pink and blue
Whisk in a jar of loyalty
A sprinkle of rudeness
A pinch of spice

A dip of me being respectful
A spoonful of sloths, fish and llamas
A bowl of cheetahs speed
A dip dash of goofiness
A sprinkle of loudness
And finally a hand full of confidence.

Mia Robinson (10)
Easington Colliery Primary School, Easington Colliery

It's The Fantastic Me!

I love art and I have a big heart.
I love cats but I hate wearing hats
I don't cheat, I just listen to the beat
I adore animals
My mom thinks I'm a cannibal

I love to care about having short hair
I have never seen a bear as tough as a chair
I'm not perfect but I'll try
I will never say goodbye
I'm strong so I will listen to the song
I am brave, I'm going into the cave
No one can stop me, I will always be me
Push me down but I'll push back
Proudly stepping through the cracks
I am a cancer and people say I'm a dancer
I'm very dramatic and I'm always sympathetic
I don't live in a cave, well, that's what they say

Megan O'Neil (10)
Easington Colliery Primary School, Easington Colliery

This Is Me

How are you? My name is Genevieve
My favourite thing is Christmas Eve
I have a very pure mind
People also say I'm very kind
My singing helps all my worries leave

My favourite colour is orange
I hope I go to a good college
I fancy education
I've been to a train station
I despise mushy stuff called porridge

I always sing when I'm alone
I eat ice cream with my own cone
My brother is autistic
Also drives me ballistic
I've never met people on the throne

My favourite animal is mythical
It's one million per cent magical
It's called a unicorn
It has a golden horn
In my opinion, it's fantastical.

Genevieve Sullivan (11)
Easington Colliery Primary School, Easington Colliery

This Is Me

It has armour on its back
If you get close you'll get a whack
It has more than one horn
Each bigger than a thorn
An armoured beast it may be
It has the characteristics of me
It can live in safaris and zoos
And it'll do a lot of poos
It is super protective
And certainly not a detective
It can get mad
And they can come from Chad
It loves to eat grass
But it hates class
They can be female or male
And come with a tail
It is super strong
But sometimes it can be wrong
It can be vigilant
And see a small ant

It is super brave
Only a few have ever seen a wave
They can be long
Even some can sing a song
They can be danger
To any stranger.

Connor Morrow (10)
Easington Colliery Primary School, Easington Colliery

This Is Me

I have lots of friends
They are all tens
Newcastle is the best
Maxi on the wing skins the rest
Football I like to play
Drawing is the way

My Xbox is great
For school, I'm never late
Sleeping I like to do
Also cooking, especially stew
Pasta tastes like heaven
My favourite number is eleven

I love the colour green
Many people around me are mean
But I don't let them put me down
I live in a cool town
I like talking a lot because I am loud
Their words won't shut me out because I'm proud
In the steps of success, I'm still climbing the wall
Never will I fall

I will reach the top
And I will never stop
Or will I?

Noah B (11)
Easington Colliery Primary School, Easington Colliery

My Name Is Bobby

My name is Bobby
This is my family hobby
There is more than one
So let this intro be gone
I like darts
I hope to be top of the charts
My favourite colour is green
My mom likes to clean
My dad works so hard
For his birthday I get him a card
My dog, Hunter, is very loud
Still, I am proud
My other puppy is so cute
But compared to Hunter he is minute
My nana is so old
I'm surprised she's not covered in mould
Now for my hobbies
In gaming, I'm put into lobbies
I like swimming
I love winning

I like to play pool
Some may consider me cool.

Bobby Chilton (10)
Easington Colliery Primary School, Easington Colliery

Little Me

Play left back and left wing
Can bend like a worm
After sports, I like a hot bath that burns
I play football and cricket, gymnastics too
Not a big fan of Iron Bru

I love spaghetti
Can be louder than a yeti
And love eating burgers at the Dancing Betty
Don't lie when I say I love confetti

Have 21 friends
And love building dens
But love the taste of juicy cooked hens

I'm a cancer
Quite a good dancer

Been to Africa, Cuba, Turkey and Greece
Feel warm wearing a fleece
And adore the taste of all meats.

Mason Fox (10)
Easington Colliery Primary School, Easington Colliery

This Is Me

Anxiety, you will need a lot
Brave, you will need a whole pot
Crazy, you can't make me without it
Defensive, you will need a little bit
Extrovert, that's me
Flexible, used to be
Goofy, you will need a lot of that
Happy, just like Postman Pat
Independent, you will need a teaspoon full
Jokey, I could possibly give that a pull
Kind, all of the time
Laughter, is my constant chime
Moody, not at all
Noisy, I'm appalled
Outstanding, as much as a pea
Phoebe Harrison, this is me.

Phoebe Harrison (11)
Easington Colliery Primary School, Easington Colliery

This Is Me

I'm a footballer
A dog walker
A Sunderland supporter
A Westlife singer
A listener
A dreamer

To make me, you will need:
A dash of craziness
Shorts
A football
Happiness
Respect
Ten minutes of relaxation
Family

My name is Dan
And my friends are so cool
I love to go to school
And I love to go to the pool
My name is Dan
And my friend is Archie

He's mint
My friend is Rhys
And he is mint
My friend is Lewie
And he is mint
They are my best friends
How about you?

Daniel W (10)
Easington Colliery Primary School, Easington Colliery

This Is Me

How to make me:
A tub of lazy
A sprinkle of joy
An ounce of sleep
Cold cheese pasta
1ml of online games
A cup of relaxation

How to bake:
First, mix a tub of lazy with a sprinkle of joy until silky smooth
Next, sprinkle the cold cheese pasta all over the mixture
Next, add an ounce of sleep and mix with a cup of relaxation
Once mixed so it's smooth again, put 1ml of online games
Cook for thirty minutes
Once cooked, leave out for twenty minutes to cool
Then enjoy!

Lacey Jane Scott (11)
Easington Colliery Primary School, Easington Colliery

How To Make Kayla/Me

Before we start, you need a cooking pot
After you've got it, you need three cups of kindness
Then one cup of angry
Then a lot of smart
Then ten cups of awesome
Now you need to mix it
Now two cups of curious
Then one and a half cups of happy
Then five cups of family
Then twenty cups of silly
Lots of cups of the colour orange
The last thing is fun... so, eight cups of fun
Mix it again
And put it in the oven now for thirty seconds.

Kayla Fergus (10)
Easington Colliery Primary School, Easington Colliery

This Is Me

I am so kind
I've got a mathematical mind
But I despise mice
Can't you tell I'm so nice?
I am so funny
Can't you tell I've got a lot of money?
I support Liverpool
Don't they rule?
I am so cool
I can take a joke
I really like Coke
Football is my favourite sport
My best friend said he is really, really short
But I am a brother
From another mother
Hoped you liked my rap
Oh, let me just run my last four laps!

Finlay (10)
Easington Colliery Primary School, Easington Colliery

This Is Me

My dad was in the army and I want to be in the army
It is my dream to join the army
It would help my life
I have been trying so hard to go into the army
I still have a long time to go
When I go in the army with my dog named Pete
I love Pete and he loves me too
I need to finish school so I can be free
First I need to go to college and I need to do maths
I can push hard to achieve my goal to go into
the army.

Jayden D (10)
Easington Colliery Primary School, Easington Colliery

This Is Me

Football is my favourite sport,
I like to play with my small ball.
I kick the ball with my left foot,
Like no one has ever kicked it before.
Sometimes it hits the crossbar,
But then I score,
It enters the large goal,
Rolling back like a fat hairy mole!
I'm like a ninja,
My moves are skilful,
My moves are fast,
No one can catch me
Because I am class!

Layton (11)
Easington Colliery Primary School, Easington Colliery

This Is Me

- **G** ood grader by the end of school because that's really cool
- **E** very day I stand out, now I am here to shout it out
- **R** esilience is my middle name and I am pretty good at board games
- **B** eautiful and a little mischievous but soon I will get what I want to achieve
- **I** know Barack Obama is sweet as a farmer
- **L** ove my family now this poem ends happily.

Sophie D (11)
Easington Colliery Primary School, Easington Colliery

Mixed Emotions

My anger is trapped in my deepest thoughts
I feel lonely with the best of friends
Who am I?

People say I am a happy normal girl
I'm held down by over-thinking
Who am I?

My teeth are weird
But my friends like me the way I am
They made me giggle at the darkest moments
They don't mention my annoying habits
They stop me from feeling doubt
They're my best friends
And they made me, me.

Lilly Mae Robinson (11)
Easington Colliery Primary School, Easington Colliery

This Is Me

TikTok makes me dance a lot
I love PE when we do squats
I love the Tudor reign
Which gets me a bigger brain
I like to take hard football shots

I'm fearless and bold
I'm always very cold
I like to go on walks
And like to drink Coke
I like to be happy a lot

My confidence is low
But I know I have time to grow
My favourite colour is blue
And I love a nice view
My sis is so slow.

Lilly-May Pearson (11)
Easington Colliery Primary School, Easington Colliery

This Is Me

Recipe for my special cake:
First, measure out some happiness to start the bake
Then, add a pinch of creativity to add something special to the cake
Next, add some brightness and for about ten seconds, let it be
Mix it with a spoonful of messiness to make it sound like me
Put it in the oven for an hour and a half
Once it's out, decorate it with sweetness, kindness, and clumsiness.

Evie Wilson (10)
Easington Colliery Primary School, Easington Colliery

This Is Me

I am like a super maths mind
It's my time to shine
I'm always on the grind
I always wear fabric
Let me work my mysterious magic
Football is my favourite sport
To let you know I am really really short
Maths gives me pain
English drives me insane
Blood runs through my veins
I am optimistic
I want to be artistic
I am cool
I don't want to be a fool
Can't you see
This is me?

Declan B (11)
Easington Colliery Primary School, Easington Colliery

Guess The Cricket Team

Although we play cricket
We don't seem to hit the wicket
Even in games like the ashes
Our team still crashes

Although our opponents have giant spiders
We are not good fighters
Somehow we won the World Cup
But now we are out of luck

Although our team suck
We didn't used to be sittin' ducks
We have a good football team
But our cricket team is not supreme
What team is it?

Logan A (10)
Easington Colliery Primary School, Easington Colliery

This Is Me

T ango Ice Blasts are like my child
H e may be a puppet, but I'm obsessed with Elmo
I love designing Dino Masks

I 'm a monkey when it comes to climbing
S cary things, I love them surprisingly I don't get scared

M y happy place is Disneyland, of course
E lvis Presley truly is king!

Hollie (10)
Easington Colliery Primary School, Easington Colliery

This Is Me

The recipe for me:
10oz of cats
A pinch of mischief
A slice of warm cheesy pizza
3kg of TV
A dash of action
50g of adventure
1g of fear
Two keyboards and mice
50g of Roblox

First, you need to mix well
Then add the Roblox carefully
After that, pour the liquid into the oven
Then sprinkle on the mischief and fear
This is me!

Aidan C (10)
Easington Colliery Primary School, Easington Colliery

This Is Me

My name is Stewart and I am very caring
And I do not mind sharing
I like to read books
And I like the way my mam cooks

My favourite animal is a fish
They sleep in water in a dish
I really like meatballs and pasta
But my friend tells me it's a disaster
I love to play outside with friends
But all they like to do is make dens.

Stewart (11)
Easington Colliery Primary School, Easington Colliery

Do You Want To Hear A Riddle?

I have blonde hair
I love to care
I will help another in need
I don't like to read
I love me
I have never been stung by a bee
I love food
It brightens my mood
I don't like to be messy
I am very dressy
I love history
I am a true mystery
I am a Capricorn
I have been me since I was born
Who am I?

Answer: Me.

Ruby (11)
Easington Colliery Primary School, Easington Colliery

How To Bake Me

Before we start, grab a pot
Add two drizzles of weirdness
Secondly, five tons of kindness
After that, six pots of cleverness
Now, two pints of funniness
Next, stir in one pot of silliness
Now for the last part
Seven drizzles of messiness

Okay, now put the pot in the oven and voila...
That's me!

Mason W (11)
Easington Colliery Primary School, Easington Colliery

This Is Me

How to make a Tyler smoothie!
Grab a bowl of acting
Add a bowl of acting
Sprinkle a handful of funniness
Pour a gallon of craziness
Add a sprinkle of climbing skill
Shake a little love for purple
Shuffle, shuffle...
Stir, stir...
And...
Poof!
That's how you make a Tyler smoothie
This is me.

Tyler Gallagher (10)
Easington Colliery Primary School, Easington Colliery

This Is Me

I am me
I love me
I want to become a vet
I would like to have a dog
Or maybe even a hog
I have lots of friends
And none of them offends
I have lots of fun
I can even make a good pun
I have a big family
And we play quite happily
I really like drawing
I do a lot of yawning
Cute as I can be
I am me!

Olivia K (11)
Easington Colliery Primary School, Easington Colliery

Me

I hate eating a big part of cheese
But I love eating a lot of green peas
I have a tiny dog
Who gets lost in the fog
I see a lot of bees and I have hairy knees

I am a big bunch of fun
And my dog is kinda my son
I am a bit tall
But I can't kick a ball
I broke my ankle... I can't run.

Riley Foster (11)
Easington Colliery Primary School, Easington Colliery

This Is Me

One pinch of sassy
Two cups of funny
1tbsp of athletic
Four drips of clumsy
1/2 spoon of pretty
3% artistic
Nine cups of friendly
Ten jugs full of good fashion

Stir to make me
Special, kind, forgiving
Whisk it well
Do not make an unforgettable spell
Stir it well... to make me.

Aaliyah Brown (10)
Easington Colliery Primary School, Easington Colliery

This Is Me

To create me, you need:
1oz of fun
A pinch of happiness
1 gram of mischief
A dash of action

Now you need to:
First, add the ounce of fun
Next, stir the 3kg of happiness
After that, add the dash of action
Finally, add 1g of mischief
Bake until the brightness comes alive
This makes me.

Rhys M (11)
Easington Colliery Primary School, Easington Colliery

This Is Me

My dog, what a brilliant thing
His birthday is 1st April
His name is Boris
Boris was as naughty as a bull
He is as fluffy as a furball
He is a really big drama queen
He is a scardey-cat because he is scared of water
He is a large dog and he is giant
Now how will you describe yourself?

Emmi (11)
Easington Colliery Primary School, Easington Colliery

This Is Me

I am as cold as ice
My friends are really nice
I play on Fortnite
And I play it all night
I play football
With my best ball
I ride on my cool bike
While wearing Nike
I am a parkour master
When I get faster
I love running
While making pudding
I play on my tank
When making a prank.

Callum Fishburn (11)
Easington Colliery Primary School, Easington Colliery

This Is Me

D elightful boy who helps anyone
E xtravagant person who is really friendly
C an we be friends?
L et's play football and include everyone
A nd be yourself and never criticise
N ever put yourself down.

Declan C (11)
Easington Colliery Primary School, Easington Colliery

This Is Me

K ind-hearted to everyone I see
R eading is my bad enemy
Y ou are cute and special
S afe all day and night
T alk all day to people
A rtistic drawer and creative
L ove everyone in the world.

Krystal Ward (10)
Easington Colliery Primary School, Easington Colliery

This Is What Makes Me!
A kennings poem

I am a...
Meat eater
McDonald's consumer
Super-star striker
Determined defender
Cricket watcher
Late riser
Humour spreader
Sweet eater
Pancake maker
Sibling controller
Heavy sleeper
Phone watcher
Tango Ice Blast drinker
And finally...
A good friend.

Olivia Cockfield (10)
Easington Colliery Primary School, Easington Colliery

My Little Hunter Friend

My little hunter friend
It lives in the dessert strange and scary
The Usain Bolt of the arachnid world
Part spider, part scorpion
A deadly hunter
And a mincer
What is it?

Answer: A camel spider.

Jaxon (10)
Easington Colliery Primary School, Easington Colliery

This Is Me

With a sprinkle of silliness
And a crack of friends
A teaspoon of school
A cup of family
And a sprinkle of kindness
An ounce of food and there you go
You have created me.

Josh C (11)
Easington Colliery Primary School, Easington Colliery

Happy

H appiness is when I play games
A nd I love my parents
P arents spend time with me
P eppa Pig is not a good show
Y eah, that's me.

Bruce Langlands (10)
Easington Colliery Primary School, Easington Colliery

This Is Me

I am...
A footballer
A gamer
A reader
A pizza eater
A listener
A sleeper
A dreamer
A writer
A typer
A spyer
A cake lover
A runner
A player
A baker
A whistle-blower
A boxer.

Kenzie B (11)
Easington Colliery Primary School, Easington Colliery

This Is Me
A kennings poem

I am a...
Food eater
A clothes maker
Dog owner
Auntie forever
Youngest family member
Animal lover
Someone who wants to be a police officer
Hair designer
Angry person
Stressed human.

Ella R (11)
Easington Colliery Primary School, Easington Colliery

I Am A...
A kennings poem

I am a...
Chocolate eater
Positive dreamer
Watermelon lover
Good helper
Spider fleer
Light sleeper
Outstanding painter
Slow runner
Great organiser
Amazing baker
Hard worker.

Kayla C (11)
Easington Colliery Primary School, Easington Colliery

Make Me With...

Make me with:
Ten scoops of madness
99 grams of kindness
Five litres of sportiness
A scoop of angriness
1.5 litres of hungriness
One gallon of messiness.

Jake Oliver (10)
Easington Colliery Primary School, Easington Colliery

I Am Me
A kennings poem

I am a ...
Horse rider
Pony lover
Book reader
Pancake maker
Late riser
Sleep lover
Heat lover
Cheese scoffer
Good helper
And finally...
A good friend.

Lily May (10)
Easington Colliery Primary School, Easington Colliery

This Is What Makes Me, Me
A kennings poem

I am a...
Brownie eater
Cookie maker
Coke drinker
Ice breaker
Horror gamer
Art drawer
Summer lover
Heavy sleeper
And finally...
Great friend haver.

Kai (11)
Easington Colliery Primary School, Easington Colliery

The Crazy Girl Nora

N ever liked maths
O bsessed with curry
R aces siblings to fridge
A nd I have the best friends and family.

Nora (10)
Easington Colliery Primary School, Easington Colliery

Only Me
A kennings poem

I am a...
Good defender
Rugby player
Super striker
Deep sleeper
Crisp eater
Summer lover
Football watcher
PlayStation player
Yup, that's me.

Jenson Price (11)
Easington Colliery Primary School, Easington Colliery

This Is Me
A kennings poem

I am a...
Chocolate eater
Organised dreamer
Great walker
Watermelon eater
Maths master
History interester
Cobra Kai watcher
Rollerblader.

Amii Louise W (10)
Easington Colliery Primary School, Easington Colliery

I Am A...
A kennings poem

I am a...
Nice footballer
Chocolate eater
Phone watcher
Good dodgeballer
Fast runner
Great winner
Water lover
This is me!

Ryan Pine (10)
Easington Colliery Primary School, Easington Colliery

This Is Me
A kennings poem

Food lover
Fashion designer
Big brainer
Food maker
Favourite daughter
Joker
Good sister
Sleeper
Organiser
Dreamer.

Layla E (10)
Easington Colliery Primary School, Easington Colliery

I Am Me

Unexpected
I thought I was tiny
Compared to all my classmates
They're so tall
Anyway

My favourite subject is maths
But it's a bit monotonous
At times

I like English, maths and PE
They're fun
Unlike art and rugby
I despise them
Especially rugby

I love football
Just like Ronaldo
He's my favourite
Let's go, Ronaldo!

He scores goals
Unlike me
I've not got good accuracy
Sometimes I do
Sometimes I score screamers
Me?
I know
I'm just such a beamer!

At home I have drums
And a piano
I know, right!
So cool
It's so fun
And I'm just so joyful
When I play

I'm decent at piano
Not so much for drums
Only on the initial grade
It's a bit dumb
On the piano

I'm grade 1
I'm quite happy with the way I've done!

I've got an optimistic life
For when I'm older
I want my own plane
Cessna 182
My preference

I want to be a dentist
Just like my parents
It'll be soo fun
And great!
I could travel the world
In my plane
It'll be so fun
And I'll enjoy it
However
In order to do this
I have to study hard
And achieve a lot.
My dad's motto is:
"Work hard, play hard!"

Evangelos Pappas (10)
Loretto Junior School, Musselburgh

Just Me

When I grow up, I want to travel the globe
When I grow up, I want to help the young generation have a better world to grow up in
When I grow up, I want to help dyslexic children

When I was young, I jumped in puddles of mud
When I was young, I played hide-and-seek behind old trees
When I was young, I had tea parties with toy animals

But that was in the past and that is in the future
We live in the present so let's focus on that

Right now, I feel happiness running through me like a galloping horse
Other times sometimes I feel sadness trudging all over me
Sometimes I jump up and down with joy
And sometimes I yell into my pillow, anger running through my veins

Now I've talked enough, so what about you?

Rose Adams (10)
Loretto Junior School, Musselburgh

When I'm Older

When I'm older
I will go to work every day
Then I will go inside for my day to begin
Then I will go right back home for my day to almost end
And then I will say, "Home, sweet home."
I will have a beautiful cat, one dog, two tortoises, two horses
And one ferret, that would mean I'd have seven pets.

When I'm older
I will do my daily routine
For example, I will feed my pets, clean out their cages
Then I will let them run around for a while in the garden
My horses will be in a field, not the garden
And my tortoises will be in a cage, not roaming around free
Or else I will not be able to spot them

When I'm older
I will travel to places
But still have a house
I will have a map of the world
And I will pin down all the places I have been to
China, Japan, Spain, France, Romania
There are a few other places
But I have listed a few I have already been to

When I'm older
I want to be a vet
I mean, sometimes blood and everything creeps me out
But at the end of the day, you would feel like a hero
For saving all those sick animals

When I'm older
The type of hobbies I will like is quite hard to tell
But I guess my hobbies would be art, sewing, horse riding
Reading and writing things.

Ava Shanks (10)
Loretto Junior School, Musselburgh

How I Feel

I don't really feel like myself today
We have to do our Burns' poems
These are some of the things that I love and hate
I love hockey
I love playing it with my team
There are hard teams we play
I put a lot of effort into training
So does the team
And we are all determined to win
Maths is my favourite academic subject
It is interesting
Injections are my biggest dread
I panic every time I get one, it is ghastly

When I grow up, I would love to be a Scottish rugby player
Then a commentator
After that, I would love to be an accountant
Rugby is an amazing game
It helps take all your anger out in a controlled way
My favourite bit about rugby is rucking

I play for three different clubs
My favourite player is Hamish Watson

I play the bagpipes
They are super tricky
I struggle with memorising songs
My great grampa used to be the best bagpiper in the world.

Hamish Fergusson (10)
Loretto Junior School, Musselburgh

I Love Chicken Nuggets

I love chicken nuggets
They're crunchy and light
The chicken is so soft
On the very inside

I love chicken nuggets and chips
It's like ham and cheese
Though, I always leave some spare for my dog
Who never says please

I love chicken nuggets with chips and sauce
And a massive ice cream
Fit for a boss

I love ice cream
It's so creamy and light
But, you know
Lemon sorbet
So sour is just right

I love ice cream with sprinkles
They're the creamy crunch
But my mum always wants some...
"Here we go again..."

I love ice cream with sprinkles and sauce
But by then
I've got indigestion.

Charlotte Gordon (10)
Loretto Junior School, Musselburgh

This Is Me Poem

We all are different in amazing ways
Let me show you my life

I love rugby because my dad used to be a rugby player
He got me into playing rugby, now I love rugby
I have a little sister called Chloe
I love her very much
But she sometimes annoys me
And I have a mum and dad
I love them very much too
My sister is 7 years old
My mum is 36 years old
My dad is 40 years old
And I am 10 years old
My dog is 13 in human years
But in dog years he is 91.

I love to learn some things at school
I'm in P6
A question I get asked a lot of times is

What do you want to be when you're older?
I say a rugby player every year.

Lucas Teague (10)
Loretto Junior School, Musselburgh

I Don't Feel Like Myself Today

I don't feel like myself today
I don't feel like me
I don't feel emotions
I don't feel life
I don't feel adrenaline
I don't feel anything!

I don't feel like myself today
I don't feel like a human
I don't feel normal
All I feel is nothingness
Which is new to me
Normally I'm always busy
Normally I'm always active
But today
Is different somehow!

I never want to be lazy
But today
Somehow, I feel I am
The battle against life is difficult
But it can be beaten!

I don't feel like myself today
I don't feel like me!

Murray Allister (11)
Loretto Junior School, Musselburgh

Bracken's Information

I used to live in New Orleans, Lousiana, USA

To start off with
I'm going to say what jobs I want when I'm older
The jobs I desire are a landscape architect
Fashion designer
And for a side, job a chameleon breeder

The subjects I relish are art and drama
The subjects I despise are PE and games

My favourite animals are
Chameleons
Cats
Frogs
And octopi

When I'm older, I am going to go to college
With my friend, Pheobe in New Orleans

This is my about me poem
And without these thoughts and things
I wouldn't be me.

Bracken Kirk (11)
Loretto Junior School, Musselburgh

This Is Me

I play rugby all day and night
I also think I am quite nice
But I do not feel good today
I am not feeling normal
I am feeling a bit strange

I play tons of sport
Sport is the best
But sometimes you need to have a bit of a rest
But they might not always be the best
But you need a rest every now and then
But now I am bored of writing
I just want to stop

I am so close
I can't wait to finish
And here I am finishing
Eventually.

Ewan Kay (11)
Loretto Junior School, Musselburgh

I Could Be...

I have lots of stuff
That I want to do
So here's a list of things
That could give you a clue

I could be in a rocket
Heading up to space
Or drifting in a car
Winning a big race

I could be an acrobat
Working for the circus
Walking on the tightrope
Would become my purpose

I could live in a castle
I would sit on a huge throne
But all the royal duties
Would really make me groan

I could be a rockstar
The guitar I would shred
But I'm not doing any
'Cause I'm writing this instead!

Megan Hill (10)
Loretto Junior School, Musselburgh

I Am Me

My life, my story
My life is how I represent myself
My past has made me who I am today

I know what sadness feels like
I know what happiness feels like
I know what suffering feels like
I know what relief feels like

I have started to figure my future out
Decided what I want to be
I want to race horses
A jockey, that's what I want to be
Inspire the young
Like people inspired me

I am me
I am Kitty.

Kitty Strang-Steel (11)
Loretto Junior School, Musselburgh

Me

I'm ten
And I really like horse riding
I've been riding for years

When I grow up
I dream of having my own stables
And riding every day

When I grow up
I want to compete for Britain in show jumping

These are my dreams
But right now, I'm just ten
So I still have dreams.

Francesca Jones (10)
Loretto Junior School, Musselburgh

Who Is Lilly?

A fabulous, fantastic, fashionista
Curly-haired
Freckled-faced
Crystal-blue-eyed girl
A sensational sparkling star
Life-laughing
Art-loving

If Lilly were the weather
She would be the bright shining sun

Who is Lilly?

It is me!

Lilly Varley (9)
Our Lady of Perpetual Succour Primary School, Widnes

Who Is George?

He is a seamless, sneaky, slithering, sportsman
As exciting as a cup final game
He's an Everton fan
A very funny man

He's a...
Titanic-lover
History-reader

If George were the weather
He'd be a dark stormy night
If George were a country
He'd be England big and bright
If George were an Olympic event
He'd be the javelin
With his sharp personality.

Who is George?

It is me!

George Connor (10)
Our Lady of Perpetual Succour Primary School, Widnes

Who Is Ewan?

He is a football kicking action-packed player
As annoying as a sassy seagull
As fast as a determined greyhound
Who never stops running

If Ewan were the weather
He would be lighting that's faster than sound
If Ewan were a blanket
He would be cosy, comforting and warm

He is outdoor-crafting
Dog-admiring
Faithful friend

Who is Ewan?

It is me!

Ewan Ainsworth (10)
Our Lady of Perpetual Succour Primary School, Widnes

Who Is Clayton?

He is a fantastic, fabulous, funny, footballer
As loyal as a lion
As fast as a flash of electric lightning

If he were the weather
He would be a thunderous storm
If he were a country
He would be magnificent Mexico
If he were an Olympic event
He would be a 100m running event
Because he sprints at six times the speed of light

Who is Clayton?

It is me!

Clayton Tomlinson (10)
Our Lady of Perpetual Succour Primary School, Widnes

Who Is Bobby?

He is a skilful loving footballer
As ferocious as a lion
As fast as a comet from out of space

If Bobby were the weather
He would be a hot hurricane
If he were a country
He would be marvellous Mexico for the spicy sunshine
If he were an animal
He would be a Great British Bulldog

TikTok-loving
Cheerful chilling

Who is Bobby?

It is me!

Bobby Abbott (9)
Our Lady of Perpetual Succour Primary School, Widnes

Who Is Louie?

He is a sensational, stupendous, super soccer star
As quick as a lightning bolt
As lively as a flying Liverpool fan
A beaming ball of light power
Delightful dog walker
Vibrant videogamer

Who is Louie?

It is me!

Louie Gore (9)
Our Lady of Perpetual Succour Primary School, Widnes

Who Is Brooke?

She is an amazingly, cool, awesome artist
Very loyal and kind as a cat

If she were an animal
She would be a crusty crab
If she were the weather
She would be sensational, smiling sunshine

TikTok-making
Roblox- winning
With a baby brother mess-creating
As silly as a happy horse
A fun-loving faithful friend

Who is Brooke?

It is me!

Brooke Burrows (9)
Our Lady of Perpetual Succour Primary School, Widnes

Who Is Lucas?

He is a fantastic, fabulous, ferocious, footballer
As fast as a ten-year-old when their mum tells them to get to bed!
A top-of-the-range latest edition FIFA deluxe

Fortnite-playing
Assist-creating

If Lucas was an Olympic event
He would be a hurdler
Because he's got springs in his heels
And can leap to the moon!

Who is Lucas?

It is me!

Lucas Campbell (10)
Our Lady of Perpetual Succour Primary School, Widnes

Who Is Daisy?

She is a skilful, strong, superb, swimmer
As kind as a playful puppy
A popular, perky, proud person

If Daisy were the weather
She would be life-giving, torrential rain
Because she adores water

If Daisy were a snake
She would be a python

She is a...
Delightful-dancer
TikTok-maker
Fun-creator

Who is Daisy?

It is me!

Daisy Roche (9)
Our Lady of Perpetual Succour Primary School, Widnes

Who Is Charlie?

He is an amazing, extravagant, awesome, artist
As mess-making as a million monsters

If Charlie were the weather
He'd be an earthquake
Since he's chaotically crazy
And sometimes mightily moody
If Charlie were a school subject
He'd be art

He is a...
Confidence-creater
Devious-drawer

Who is Charlie?

It is me!

Charlie Capewell (10)
Our Lady of Perpetual Succour Primary School, Widnes

Who Is Ethan G?

A ridiculous reader
A watchful, observant writer
A hungry hare
A marvellous mechanic
A diamond drawer

If Ethan were an animal
He would be an energetic, gymnastic, hungry hare
If Ethan were a gamer
He would sometimes graciously quit...
But at other times he would be the glorious victor

Who is Ethan G?

It is me!

Ethan G (9)
Our Lady of Perpetual Succour Primary School, Widnes

Who Is Jasmine?

She is a purposeful piano player
Sometimes as calm as a drifting cloud
Other times, as sparkling as a sensational star

If she were a country
She'd be Thailand
Exotic, entrancing
Showing where she's from

Anime-lover
Astonishing-artist
Arching-Sagittarius

Who is Jasmine?

It is me!

Jasmine Winders (10)
Our Lady of Perpetual Succour Primary School, Widnes

Who Is Jack?

He is a stupendous scientist
As intelligent as a dolphin
A brilliant, brainstorming, brain cell
A marvellous mathematician

If Jack were an animal
He'd be a giraffe
Because he is terrifically tall

Platypus-loving
Day-dreaming
Freckle-faced
Idea-creating

Who is Jack?

It is me!

Jack Butler (10)
Our Lady of Perpetual Succour Primary School, Widnes

Who Is Toby?

He is a superstar, skilful, sensational, soccer hero
As loyal as a lion
A speedy shooting star

If he were the weather
He would be crazy wind or wonderful wind
Because he can sometimes be strong and angry
Or at other times, calm and still

Max-relaxing
Computer-gaming

Who is Toby?

It is me!

Toby Sinclair (9)
Our Lady of Perpetual Succour Primary School, Widnes

Who Is Erin?

She is a speedy, skilful, sensational, superstar soccer player
As kind as a cuddly, fluffy, teddy bear
An energetic flash of electric lightning

If Erin were an Olympic event
She would be slalom skiing
Because she is fast and furious

Daydreaming
Goal-scoring

Who is Erin?

It is me!

Erin Tyrer (10)
Our Lady of Perpetual Succour Primary School, Widnes

Who Is Erin?

She is a happy, harmless, hard-working horse-rider
As strong as the most powerful stallion
A beautiful baking star

If Erin were the weather
She would be a bright, sunny, summer day
If Erin were a season
She would be spring

Horse-handling
Cake-creating

Who is Erin?

It is me!

Erin Dourley (10)
Our Lady of Perpetual Succour Primary School, Widnes

Who Is Lexie?

She is a great, generous, gymnast
As kind as a koala
She is as flexible and fascinating as a swan

If Lexie were the weather
She would be gently swirling snowflakes
Because she's calm and unique

TikTok-creating
Gymnast-loving

Who is Lexie?

It is me!

Lexie Dwyer (10)
Our Lady of Perpetual Succour Primary School, Widnes

Who Is Sam?

He is a great, gorgeous, glory-seeking gamer
As proud as a huge dazzling lion
A twinkling star in the sky

If Sam were the weather
He'd be speedy sparkly snow

He is a...
Toy-playing
Animal-loving
Citizen of tomorrow

Who is Sam?

It is me!

Sam Turpin (10)
Our Lady of Perpetual Succour Primary School, Widnes

Who Is Niamh?

She is as nice as a new neighbourhood nine-year-old
As shy as a mischievous meerkat
As sparkling as a star in the midnight misting sky

Milkshake-making
Xbox-gaming

If Niamh were an animal
She would be a playful puppy

Who is Niamh?

It is me!

Niamh Collins (9)
Our Lady of Perpetual Succour Primary School, Widnes

Who Is Billy?

He is a phenomenal, precise, poised,
playful, pianist
As strong as a snake
A sparkling star

If Billy were a frog
He would be tiny and yellow, with eager eyes
He'd eat lots of flies!

A fish-lover
Dog-hugger

Who is Billy?

It is me!

Billy Purcell (9)
Our Lady of Perpetual Succour Primary School, Widnes

Who Is Ethan?

Ethan is a fantastic, flying, fast, footballer
As wise as an owl
A speedy sparkling star

If Ethan were an Olympic event
He would be a high-jumper
Because he can leap as high as Snowdonia!

Goal-scorer
Joke-maker

Who is Ethan?

It is me!

Ethan Fox (10)
Our Lady of Perpetual Succour Primary School, Widnes

Who Is Charlie?

He is a fun time, precious, playful boy
As brave as a lion

He is a...
Computer-loving
Generous gamer

If he were the weather
He would be the wild wind
Because he is a wicked energetic person

Who is this mess-making machine?

It is me!

Charlie Edwards (9)
Our Lady of Perpetual Succour Primary School, Widnes

Who Is Savannah?

She is a fantastic female fighter...
Tie-breaker
Fast-knocking
Hard-working
Enemy-attacking
Buddy-defending

As fast as liquid lightning
As friendly as a frog sprinting through the summer fields

Who is Savannah?

It's me!

Savannah Fitzpatrick (9)
Our Lady of Perpetual Succour Primary School, Widnes

Who Is James?

He is an amazing, abstract, artist
As brave as a bull
As quick as a fascinating flash of lightning

If James were the weather
He'd be the sun... positive and warm

Football-defender
Video game-player

Who is James?

It is me!

James Shields (10)
Our Lady of Perpetual Succour Primary School, Widnes

Who Is Bella?

She is a delightful, dangerous, dancing, diva
She is quiet in class, but sometimes she is fast
Her favourite animal is a giraffe

If she were the weather
She would be the sun
Because she likes being warm

Who is Bella?

It is me!

Bella Sheridan (9)
Our Lady of Perpetual Succour Primary School, Widnes

The Wonderful Day

There was a person named Franco and he was very excited
Because some of his friends were going to his house
His excitement filled with joy as he opened the door
His friends went to watch with him
And after that, they went to the garden to play any game they wanted
The game they wanted to play was football and they had fun
They went to eat after a couple of minutes and they were full
They had so much fun and they would stay for 50 more minutes
They played hide-and-seek and Franco tried to find his friends
Franco found all of his friends and they were all happy that they were there
They ate again and then played a different game which was 'Stuck in the Mud'.

Franco Anthony Alcala (9)
St Aidan's Catholic Primary Academy, Ilford

My Dreams And Myself

I am the girl with thick black hair like shadows
My light brown skin with red cheeks burn in the sunlight
I like to eat spices, although my lips turn red
And that's why I am a bit taller for my age
My teachers always give me time to think
And that's why they are the best
Everyone says I am great
But sometimes I think I am a bit cruel
I would like to be a singer and a doctor when I grow up
My eyeballs are brown and my eyebrows are black
I am nine years old
My favourite subjects are swimming, music, maths and art
In my family studying is my part
My favourite colours are pink, yellow, orange, blue and purple
My favourite animal is a peacock
I am really good at art, it's close to my heart
I love my sister because she's my life

I really like mystery
My name is Sithi.

Sithi Ghosh (14)
St Aidan's Catholic Primary Academy, Ilford

This Is A Sense Of Me

Hello, this is me
My name is Sophia
I am eight years old from 4SU
Loves/adores drawing and fried chicken
My talent is that I can eat a maximum of
Four waffles and a half in ten seconds or
a bit more
I get nostalgic sometimes, due to 2018-2020
Otamatones or pianos are the best instruments
When I smell chocolate
I have the energy to run a 50-mile radius
I love running a lot
As long as I don't have to
My hearing is okay, I'd say
I love water, milk, bubble tea and...
Oh, something is missing. Juice!
I almost forgot to say that the best book
in the world
Is 'Magicalamity' by Kate Saunders
It's so fun to read!

Sophia Russo (8)
St Aidan's Catholic Primary Academy, Ilford

Who I Am

My favourite thing to do is play football every day
I play it so much that I don't know what to say
My favourite subject is English because I like
to write
I have a favourite drink and the name is Sprite
When I'm older, I want to be an engineer
I'm in school and I am in the Grade 4 Year
My favourite thing to eat is fast food
When I'm unhappy I eat it so it changes my mood
I don't eat healthy foods all the time
There's a fruit that I don't like and the name is lime
When I go home I will eat a sugary sweet
It tastes so good that I don't know how many I eat
This is me!

Asaad
St Aidan's Catholic Primary Academy, Ilford

How Loving I Am

I am eight years old
I love helping other people and caring for others
I love helping other people
Because you have to be kind, caring and loving
It's good to help others in need
Because maybe you don't know what they're going through
And you're the one helping them
You should always be kind-hearted
I love to cheer people up
And when other people are hurt help them get back on their feet
I am a wonderful friend to have
And I hope my friends feel that way about me.

Evelina Niculae (8)
St Aidan's Catholic Primary Academy, Ilford

My Feelings

I'm unique, happy, good at football
Strong, proud and sporty
I have dark ginger hair, caring
My favourite song is Toxic
I'm good at school
Also in the swimming pool
My favourite days are Sunday and Monday
I have lots of friends that will go to the end
I am a helping person
This is me!

Lucca Pavanello (9)
St Aidan's Catholic Primary Academy, Ilford

Mayhem-Making Morgan

From the day I took my first breath
To now, I'm struggling with math
Acing tests with flying colours
But that's what I'd like to imagine

The endless possibilities of the universe are never-ending
So why not cause mayhem and become a menace
My attitude is as disgusting as a Brussels sprout
Don't forget the gravy on the side
Don't be like me or suffer the consequences
Missing lunch and breaktimes is nothing too extreme
But seeing the light of day is on a completely another level

Showing no remorse is brutal and not fatal
My mother just gives me the 'I'm not angry, just disappointed' look
But what's that going to do? Nothing
Getting kind of side-tracked, let's take time to relax
Let's take time to look at the positives, say goodbye to the negatives

Drinking coffee is what I'm known for if you're hating on McCafe's
What's wrong with you?
Tea is sweeter but bitter is where it's at!

If I were you, I recommend you try it
Enough of coffee, let's move on to my
good personality
Hysterical, adventurous, mysterious
All of that... put it all together and you get me
My friends are awesome, so let me introduce them to you
One of them is Fabulous Fiyin or Fiyin for short
Funny and ecstatic, joyful as always
Next is Powerful Peter, adventurous and cool
Also, my best friend, don't know what I'd do without him
Next is Luxurious Larrence
I say he is half-kangaroo as he jumps
He's an amazing friend, all of my friends are

So if you want to be my friend, go ahead
Believe in yourself and never give up!

Morgan Agu (10)
St Mary's Catholic Primary School, Tilbury

My Life In A Poem

This poem is about me
All the things I'll do and see
I have long curly hair
And I don't like pears
Sometimes I can be very picky
I've never met someone named Nicki

I don't like to be rude
But please don't say dude
I really like food!
My favourite is jollof rice
Especially when it has tons of spice!

I travel lots and lots!
One day I would like to meet a robot!
I get annoyed when strawberries rot!

I guess I like to read
What an understatement, puh-lease!
I get through them all in at least a week!
When I finish them, it's like getting to the peak!

If you take me to Primark
It'll be better than bleak parks
Can anyone be stronger than The Rock?

Lots of questions bombard my mind!
It is so that it wastes my time!
Why's it so hard to rhyme?

For this poem, give it a tick
As my bars are sick!
I've thoroughly enjoyed writing this
It gave me a sigh of bliss!

Dorinda Ametefe (8)
St Mary's Catholic Primary School, Tilbury

Who I Am

How life can be beautiful sometimes
Same as it can be a horror film
Some people smile as bright as the sky
Some people let out a loud cry

Hey there! I'm Marianne
This is me

I'd rather stay home reading
Others might prefer outings
I love movies, honestly, I could watch them all day
I love going to the beach, sitting on the bay

I have siblings
Gosh, they make me irate
Sometimes I'm known as distant and rude
Little do they know, I might be screwed

Yes, I can be lazy sometimes
Most of the time a bit hazy

In the future, I hope to be a criminologist
Helping stop criminals

Crime rates must go to a minimal
Same as the cash bag keeps coming in

Ooh, I love shopping
There's never too much clothing
Too bad I spend too much money
That Amazon cart just keeps enlarging

Did you enjoy learning about who I am?
I have to keep going
See you next time
Hope by then, I have more dime

Marrianne Azaka-Ekpeti (10)
St Mary's Catholic Primary School, Tilbury

The Incredulous Ife

Well, I am Ife
The boy of ten years
I will stress again and again just for a year
I am cool, epic, and super smart
I say this, deep down in my heart

My stupendous alter-ego allows me
To communicate with people of all habits and traits, see
I have cool, unfazed friends: like Larry, Harry and Peter
Sam, Sooma, Ethan, the list goes on and it never ends
Like Morgan, Alex, Fiyin and Kengah
Adam, Shanoy and Theo complete the list, yeah

As a gargantuan fan of football
I play regularly
I also study a lot, you see
So I can nourish my brain and its extraterrestrial power
Keep it fresh, hour after hour

I enjoy gaming and making raps and poems
Rocket League and Roblox and a game
called Owen

I'm Ife in year 6
And I'm in an epic fix
What secondary school
Will I go to after all?
I'm a boy with big brains and ambitions
And incredibly stupendous missions
The story of my life is complete.

Ifechukwude Emmanuel Nwaokolo (10)
St Mary's Catholic Primary School, Tilbury

I Am Harry, The Footballer

Hello, I am Harry
People call me Haribo
My friends are Peter, Ife, Ethan, Sam and Larry
And I like the lovely film Dumbo
People say I'm smart
And I say this from the heart
I like playing football

And playing in pools
I love to have a huge laugh
But not to feel ill or barf
I like people being there for me when I am sad
I despise people without manners or who are rude

With the desire for football
I play very often
I also learn in the year number 6
Full of laughs smiles and lots of know-it-alls
Gaming is one of my favourite things
I like Fortnite, Rocket League, Roblox and Overwatch

I play with my friends called Shanoy and Adam
Who always put up a good fight

Now you know me
Who I am, what I know and love
I hope you enjoyed
Just remember, this is me.

Harry Morris (11)
St Mary's Catholic Primary School, Tilbury

All About My Life

Since I'm in this school
I am feeling really cool
However, I found some friends
That sometimes were fake
They used me for clout
But now I found a new friend
Which was a girl
I've been friends with her for nine months
She makes me really jolly
We never have a fight
Or else we will break up

Sometimes I am rude
But I have a mood
And that mood is sometimes nice
But I can bring some spice

I really like food
Which is spaghetti jollof
If you bring me any
Your hands will be filled with nothing to eat!

My style is softie
I normally eat toffee
I wear skirts and trousers
Do not bring me dresses!
I like my hair in buns
But I don't like being in the sun.

Erin Asemota
St Mary's Catholic Primary School, Tilbury

The Tremendous Ethan

Hi, I am Ethan
The one and only, smart, well-mildly Ethan
Well, I am only ten years old
With a pretty average (and extremely boring) life
But someday, you will see me on the news
Rocking my cool shirt soon

Hmm, friends, I have a few
Like: Ife, Somma, Samuel
This phenomenal trio are just some of my army of friends

This is my smartest friend (mockingly smarter than me)
You might be wondering why I dedicated a verse to a friend
When you could dedicate it to yourself
Well, I don't know, I just like him

Well, the end after talking about everything I can think about
I want to make this a tremendous ending
The classic.

Titoluwanimi Tunde-Oke (10)
St Mary's Catholic Primary School, Tilbury

A Fountain Of My Dreams

When I'm older I'll be a sophisticated doctor
I'll show everyone I'm a talented singer
Listen up, people!
I'll visit different countries so I could find different species
Stop eating sweets but not delicious, chocolate Reese's
Are you still there?
Hope I'm not talking to air!
Yes, I do really care
I am very fair

Will stop violent, sad world hunger
Might help all the people in South Africa
Could be a celebrity showing a lot of creativity
Be a parent and show responsibility
Maybe a chef and cook some rice
It will definitely be very nice
Hope my dreams will come true
I hope the same for me and you.

Michelle Dongmo (9)
St Mary's Catholic Primary School, Tilbury

How My Dreams Behave When I Go To Sleep

When I go to sleep every night
All my dreams come to life
Whizzing and swirling in my head
While I'm stirring in my bed

All of the dreams in the air
Acting like they all don't care
All of them making me dizzy
While they are all very busy

All of the dreams are extremely crazy
And make me feel really hazy
All of them whispering in my ear
When my gifts are extremely near

I still don't know what the gifts are
But I will store them in my heart
My darling dreams will not let me down
And never ever make me frown

Now you see my lovely friend
All my dreams will never end.

Neytiri Sinclair (9)
St Mary's Catholic Primary School, Tilbury

When I Grow Up...

When I grow up what will I be?
Will I be a footballer
Scoring all the fantastic goals?

Will I be a doctor
Helping people get better
When they are sick?

Will I be a famous chef
Cooking lots of delicious food?

Will I be a hairdresser
Cutting the people's hair
To make them look better?

Will I be a musician
With all different types of instruments?

Will I be an astronaut
Exploring different planets
And floating through the stars?

I guess we'll have to wait and see
What I decide to be
When I grow up.

Theresa Iloene (8)
St Mary's Catholic Primary School, Tilbury

My Dream And Goals

When I go to sleep
All of my dreams float to life
My dreams start to explode
My bed starts to rise, just like my goals
My dreams are all very happy
But some are a bit crazy!

All my goals are cool
But my dreams are crazy
My dreams will never go *poof!*
My darling friends are the little dreams
The goals that I have
Are made by me!

They all like me
But crazy, crazy!
None are unhappy
Not hazy but extremely crazy!

My job would be a dream artist
Nothing would be grey
But colour is me
I love my dreams.

Precious Ogunsola (9)
St Mary's Catholic Primary School, Tilbury

All About Me

S omeone lost their joy I go and find them to ensure it's not a ploy.
M y eyes help me see anyone unhappy
A re you going to be a fake friend?
R espect is what I send
T hat's me

F ood is what I treasure
R emember I like to measure
I have a favourite food called jollof rice
E specially when you add more spice!
N ever ever will like baked beans
D on't be mean

I have not got one friend
A person like me can mend
M y body also can bend.

Rebecca Bamidele
St Mary's Catholic Primary School, Tilbury

All About Me

I shine as bright as a star
I feel like another
Just you and I
Like in my life

I need my life
My life is just a bless
I love to play
I love to try
I never give up
It is just a bless

I need my life
This is just my bribe
I need to know
What it is
This is just my life

This is all about me
This is my life
To never give up

I am a lovely person
Like a flower
I like to help people
Just like a star

I love to read
I am a breeze.

Abigail Blake (11)
St Mary's Catholic Primary School, Tilbury

When I Grow Up...

When I grow up, what will I be?
Will I be a hairdresser
Cutting all the beautiful hair?

Will I be an astronaut
Exploring different planets?
Will I be a doctor
Making people better?

Will I be a footballer
Scoring all the goals?
Will I be a zookeeper
Seeing all the moles?

Will I be a bike rider
Racing with different teams?
Will I be a firefighter
Watering all the steams?

Mara Calin (8)
St Mary's Catholic Primary School, Tilbury

Life's Little Luxuries

This is me, oh this is me
My life began, as a baby
In the early stages, I've always been winning
Been competing forever, like pieces stuck together
I shine like a diamond, in the mind
Waiting to be an Einstein

My closest friends are always there
When they are down, I'm always being a clown
We all get along like Buzz, Woody and Jessie
We stick together like puzzle pieces that never disappear.

Summer O'Brien (11)
St Mary's Catholic Primary School, Tilbury

My Dreams

My dream is to be a celebrity
So I can be famous
But there's nothing like a lamous
So I can beat the singers
There will winners

My dream is to travel
I want to win a raffle
So I can win a prize
I hope it's really nice
Then I can eat a pizza

My name is Sam
I cook with a pan
I never saw someone named Dan
I like an animal which is a lamb
But I like to eat ham.

Samantha Falusi
St Mary's Catholic Primary School, Tilbury

The Wonders Inside Me!

The wonders inside me
Good and bad, they can be
Ever since I was three
I've lacked some glee
But I can't wait to be free
Like the wonders inside me
It doesn't take a lot to find the true me

My life has been broken into two
Ever since my parents were broken into two
Restricts me from being over the moon
My life is a room
But it still blooms.

Kengah Happi (10)
St Mary's Catholic Primary School, Tilbury

Follow Your Dreams

You're never too old to follow your dreams
It is never what it seems
This is me
And I have positivity

I like art
And it has always been in my heart
Like my brother who inspired me
And I enjoyed every bit of it
As art is a part of me

Shining as bright as a star
I improve, higher and higher
You are never too old to follow your dreams.

Giselle Rowland (10)
St Mary's Catholic Primary School, Tilbury

Who Inspired Me?

M aths
I nspired me in my lesson
S miles like a sun in the blue sky like the sea
S he is a fun teacher

B loom like a poppy at a park where nobody goes
L illy petal in the Amazon river
A mazing
S marter than an information book
S ay nice comments to everyone
E xciting teacher.

Hannah Joan Blake (11)
St Mary's Catholic Primary School, Tilbury

Godadom

G - God starts with my name, even when
O - Odd stuff happens to me
D - Daddy is my father.
A - 'A' stands for 'Adom' in Ghanaian language meaning 'Grace'.
D - Does it mean my name is 'God's Grace'?
O - Of course yes and
M - Mummy is my mother.

Godadom Boafo (7)
St Mary's Catholic Primary School, Tilbury

Zap, It's Zac

This is me
As smart as I can be
This is me, as calm as I can be
This is me, as cool as I can be
This is me, as kind as I can be
This is me, as resilient as I can be
This is me, as determined as I can be
This is me, as brave as I can be.
But I know I can do better...
Because this is me.

Ayodamola Falayi (10)
St Mary's Catholic Primary School, Tilbury

This Is Me!

My life is full of ups
No, I never have downs
To be one of my class tops
I keep my face free of frowns
Living with gratitude
Is my full-time attitude
After putting in my best
To God, I leave the rest

Every day my family go higher
I won't be a liar
Shooting up to my dreams
Cause 3 x 6 is 18.

Imisioluwa Kabiawu (9)
St Mary's Catholic Primary School, Tilbury

All Of My Favourite Dreams

Some are big
Some are small
You have got to choose
'Cause you can't have them all

Some come true
Sadly some do not
A few you can remember
Most you forgot

Some are important
Others you can't live without
For some, you may have to pursue
Other people may doubt.

Samuel Oboite (9)
St Mary's Catholic Primary School, Tilbury

Nabeelah

N abeelah is my name
A lways ready to play a game
B eing an eight-year-old
E verything I'm being told
E very time I try new things
L et me see what life brings
A lways been brave and kind
H alf Polish and half Nigerian young mind.

Nabeelah Jokosanya (8)
St Mary's Catholic Primary School, Tilbury

My Favourite Things

It starts with 'F'
And it comes from a chef
It goes in your tummy
And it's oh so yummy!
What am I?
Food of course!

It starts with 'S'
And is a place for fun
You have to learn
The teachers are there
What am I?
School, of course!

Adedamola Adeyemo (8)
St Mary's Catholic Primary School, Tilbury

A House Of Favourite Things

Brown, tasty chocolate
With white, fluffy marshmallows
Fills me with joy
And enormous satisfaction

Sweet, warm popcorn
Always cracks and pops!
Jollof rice and chicken
Now I'm incredibly hungry!

Victoria-Florence Uzomah (8)
St Mary's Catholic Primary School, Tilbury

My Favorite Things

Food makes you live
Like marshmallows, biscuits, cupcakes
You shouldn't eat too much
It can make you sick

Making food really fun
Cakes are really yummy too
I like baking, it's really fun.

Temiloluwa Owoeye (9)
St Mary's Catholic Primary School, Tilbury

Seun

S ilent
E ducational
U nderstandable
N ice.

Seun Oladokun
St Mary's Catholic Primary School, Tilbury

Sola

S mart
O rganised
L ucky
A mazing.

Sola Oladokun
St Mary's Catholic Primary School, Tilbury

All About Me

My favourite colour is tortoise-green
I am not lean or mean
And I love working with a team
My hair is brown
Like a bear
My paper of happiness
Is hard to tear
I have an unrealistic dream
Of infinite in-game money
Watermelon is my favourite fruit
It is very, very yummy
My eyes are brown
Like my hair
They like looking up
Into the air
I dream of being
A great YouTuber one day
If that happens
I don't know what I'll say
I have a little brother and sister
And a big sister too

When they are bad
I don't know what to do
I love my Xbox
And my friends
My family and cat too
It's not just the Xbox
I love them all
It is just true
Sometimes I am annoying
But I'm just being me
Sometimes I am angry
But I'm just being me
A lot of the time I backchat
But I'm just being me
Other times I'm good and happy
But I'm just being me
I am happy to be real
I love being... just me.

William Forster (10)
Tweedmouth Community Middle School, Spittal

All About Me

My eyes are as green as grass
My hair is as blonde as the beach
People find me annoying
And some find me snoring
I'm as fast as a fox
This all makes sense because
It's all about me, me, me

My love for Minecraft is above all
And I hate golf from infinity and beyond
I like to play tennis and I'm as good as
Andy Murray
I have fingers that type fast
And a loving heart as big as a blossoming rose
I have feet that run fast
And a brother that attacks
This all makes sense because
It's all about me, me, me.

All my friends are kind
And so am I
My parents are caring
And so am I
Because they love me for me
This all makes sense because
It's all about me, me, me.

Casey Mole (11)
Tweedmouth Community Middle School, Spittal

Me!

I love football as much as holidays
And I cannot wait for my best days
I have hair, blonde like sand
My eyes are blue, like a blue rubber band
I'd like to be the goalie and a striker too
And when I win I scream "Woohoo!"
I love food and eat like a horse
One of my favourites is sweet curry sauce
One of the few foods I cannot eat
Is peanut butter, it is worse than stinky feet
Football is my passion, I always give my all
But I'm not that tall
I like to be boss, like an entrepreneur
I shout like a foghorn
And jump like a kangaroo
I'm strong like an ox
I support Hibs and Liverpool
And enjoy the swimming pool
I love chocolate and crisps
As long as the packets don't have huge rips.

Dylan McCleary (11)
Tweedmouth Community Middle School, Spittal

This Is Me

I've been told to write about me
I'm not perfect, I won't disagree
But I'm going to say a little about myself
I'm not amazing, but I'm as intriguing as
a bookshelf

I have mousey brown hair and blue eyes
My clothes are also very modernised
I play loads of sports
I play in all sorts of courts

I play for a rugby team
And we always win just like a dream
My football coaches call our team 'wild cats'
We usually win against all the rats

While I'm horseriding I always do jumps
I always hold my breath and get goosebumps
I play hockey and netball
I'm a sore loser all in all

But that's just me.

Faye Robertson (11)
Tweedmouth Community Middle School, Spittal

My Gamer Zone

I'm a dog lover and I'm really lazy
I'm always in the gamer zone, yeah baby
And every day I sit down on my Switch

Sometimes Minecraft, sky-blue like the mined diamonds
I'm a YouTuber, not got a plaque yet
But I'll get it soon, you bet!

Ginger no, but I'm a real hothead
One of my friends, though, is fiery red!
I wanna be 100 (still not dead)

In my gamer zone
Minecraft, Fortnite
I'm really friendly
I ain't gonna bite

Not that strong
Don't wanna' fight
Start a race
You're probably outta sight
Superpowers I want, gimme flight!

Nico McEwen (11)
Tweedmouth Community Middle School, Spittal

Me I Am Me

My friends are as sweet as sugar
I wish I was as fast as a leopard
But I am as scared as a cat
I have a brain that tries as hard as Albert Einstein

I have hair as brown as tree bark
I have fingers to tickle my little bro
I am as clumsy as a baby bird trying to fly
As you walk or run, I trip and fall
I am me just me

I am as annoying as a fly
I have eyes like glitter
I am as funny as a comedian
And have a pair of earrings
That are as pretty as diamonds

I am as slow as a snail
I am as loud as a tiger
I am as dramatic as an actor
And as creative as an artist

I am me, just me!

Bethan Doonan (10)
Tweedmouth Community Middle School, Spittal

All About Me

I like when the sun is shining on a summer's day
But I hate when the sky is grey, full of dark clouds

I am as shy as a little mouse at school
And as loud as a lion at home!
I am as annoying as a woodpecker
Going *peck, peck, peck* around my sister

No pets, though I'd like a dog
A pug with beige fur, please!
I feel fiery hot anger rising in my body when it's time for bed
I feel annoyed when people don't listen
Though I am loved by my family, friends and grandparents
I feel safe around the people I know
Like I'm always in a soft hug

I am all of this because I'm just me.

Romy Wilson (10)
Tweedmouth Community Middle School, Spittal

This Is Me

Am I fierce or am I gentle?
Am I normal or am I mental?
People can judge me, I don't care
I am unique so they can stare

I adore dogs but don't like cats
Dogs are amazing and that's that
I would love to go to the Bahamas one day
But not when the clouds are turning grey

Netball is my favourite sport
Even though I may be short
To me, family means a lot
Although we have always fought

Going on a dog walk with my friends
But in friendship, there are always bends
Do you like baking?
Because to me, it's just as dazzling as ice skating.

Seren Bird (10)
Tweedmouth Community Middle School, Spittal

That Is Just Me!

I am busy like a bee
Because that's just me

I am smart
But I'm not very good at art

I am cheeky
Sometimes sneaky

I am funny
Not as cute as a bunny

I am gentle
Bad things I do are accidental

I am silly
Outside, I like when it is chilly

I am as loud as a whale
I always follow the trail

Sometimes I'm quiet like a mouse
I have a very big house

My eyes are as blue as the sea
My hair is as brown as a tree

I am annoying
But I really enjoy it

My favourite is number three
Because that is just me!

Poppy Mcdonald (11)
Tweedmouth Community Middle School, Spittal

This Is Me

Every day is Saturday
When I wake up
Dad's making blueberry pie

I take a look in the mirror
And I've got
The perfect body
And a beautiful face

A dragon arrives
And will take me to the Grand Prix
My love for Formula One
Is like the five red lights

But really
I'm short like Yuki Tsunoda
But my family is caring
And so am I
My family is generous
And so am I
I've got good friends
And so have they

Being creative is me
Like on Minecraft

I will always love
Being me.

Caleb Punton (10)
Tweedmouth Community Middle School, Spittal

Who Am I?

Who am I? Let me think
Fun, kind, generous
A little bit annoying
(according to my sister)
Strong and brave like a lion
Determined, I always keep trying
My love for gymnastics shines, like the medals I win
My face is spread with a mischievous grin
I am an intelligent dolphin, swiftly swimming
Or perhaps a lazy sloth, who likes sleeping
I take in all with my sky blue eyes
I like to think I am quite streetwise
I dream of being an Oscar-winning actress
Although I need a bit more practice
So now you know all about me
I'm just Lexi.

Lexi Burgon (10)
Tweedmouth Community Middle School, Spittal

This Is Me

I like darts, gaming and football but golf is the best
It's a good thing to do when there is pressure on my chest
I get annoyed quickly when everyone is screaming my name
I shout when my ears are in pain

My team is Man United
They used to be real titans
I'm goofy, funny and active
I get real excited
When I hit a good shot
I'm absolutely delighted

I like Amsterdam, the windmills and the lovely food
When I'm tired, I get in a mood
You better watch out
My friends are a lethal team when we hang out.

Louis Outterson (11)
Tweedmouth Community Middle School, Spittal

This Is Me

The dinosaurs were alive
They died down
So we got down on our knees
As palaeontologists

I'll be an archaeologist
Finding unique things like me
I'm unique

Or I can be a neurologist
Finding out how we know so much
And how we recognise something

Maybe, just maybe, a biologist
I'll study humans, plants, animals
And the environment which they live in

But I'm not a stick
I'm a boulder
I'm getting older
That's me
Unique.

Damon Dobson (11)
Tweedmouth Community Middle School, Spittal

All I Want To Be Me I Me

My hair is like a chocolate bar
Plaited in pretty braids
My brain tries hard
All day long
My eyes that water when
I see stray dogs
My nose that smells
Miles of hay!
My mouth that eats
Delicious food I cook
And my lips that kiss
My problems away
All I want to be is me, me, me
I am as tall as a tree
My kindness is as big as the sea
My meanness is as small as a flea
My shyness is no bigger than a cheetah
But I am as loud as a lion
All I want to be is me, me, me.

Michalina Zielinska (11)
Tweedmouth Community Middle School, Spittal

This Is Me

Fingers that tickle my brother and sister
Legs that run every race
I can be funny when my brothers are annoying me
I am sassy, chatty and annoying
Though kind and nice
Just like my friends
When I am swimming
I am like a dolphin
I have dirty blond hair
I love gymnastics because I'm flexible
I love to be kind
Like my friends
I believe in myself
I never give up
I love my dog
My heart loves my family
Almost as much as I love McDonald's
But I do love my mum!

Charlotte Richardson (11)
Tweedmouth Community Middle School, Spittal

This Is Me

I am cool in my own way
I love to watch Neighbours every weekday!
My family are cool and fun
While I love swimming, I hate to run

My favourite pastime is watching H2O
Whilst in the winter I like to play in the snow
I like cats and cuddly kittens
When it's cold I wear fluffy mittens

At the weekend, I love to wear nice dresses
They look lovely with high heels
I have a collection of dog teddies
My favourite item is my mobile phone

This is me.

Marion Mavin (10)
Tweedmouth Community Middle School, Spittal

Me Being Me

I am as kind as a dog
As friendly as a fox
I have a good bunch of friends
Who I love lots
Like Jelly Tots

My hair is like a chocolate bar
Nice and brown
I like to hang out a lot
And upside down

I like to play football
And 8 ball pool
Me and my friends
Are very, very cool

I am as sneaky as a mouse
Getting cheese
I use my manners a lot
Please, please, please

After tea
We always play out
This is just me
Being me.

Lennox Hannan (10)
Tweedmouth Community Middle School, Spittal

This Is Just Me

I am as intelligent as a dog
As crazy as a kitten
As clumsy as a clown

I love the colour red
My annoying mouth in the morning
Is like the sky at sunset
I love chocolate and also chicken

My personality is just fine, 'cause that's just me
Feet that make me good at football
I'm as fit as a fiddle
And have eyes like a hawk

I love to sit on the couch
Watching my phone
I love England and Newcastle
But this is just me.

Luke Meakin (10)
Tweedmouth Community Middle School, Spittal

This Is Me

I am as hard as a Lego brick, but that's just me
I am as crazy as a puppy, but that's just me
I am as sporty as a footballer, but that's just me
I am as fidgety as a grasshopper, but that's just me

I am not a cat lover, that's not me
I am not a rugby lover, that's just not me
I am not an Xbox lover, that's definitely not me
I am not a person who rages that's not me

I am me.

Charlie Tait (10)
Tweedmouth Community Middle School, Spittal

All About Me!

I am as fast as a cheetah
And as funny as a clown
I am as cheeky as a monkey
And as silly as a dog

My brain works hard at everything
But I still get things wrong
I guess I'll just have to get smarter
But that's alright with me

I love to play football
But I'm not the best
I love to play rounders
Because I can hit the ball hard

That's just me, me, me.

Layton Ellis (11)
Tweedmouth Community Middle School, Spittal

This Is Who I Am

I am…

Silly as a monkey
Superstar at hockey
Tall as a giraffe
Overprotective of family
Kind to everyone and everything

Scottish and English
With a bit of Italian
A shield to my cousins
An actor at day
A gamer at night
Singer till I die

An animal lover
With a bad temper like a gorilla
Loving history as it is my jam
What can I say, this is me!

Nicole Johnson (11)
Tweedmouth Community Middle School, Spittal

This Is Me

Last day at this place
A world of stress has finally left
Now I am at a new place
Now I can start again

I have new things to see
A new adventure has begun
If I would be Spider-Man
I'd be swinging around buying cakes

If it rains
I'd be in my room playing video games
I am not mean, I am kind
I am Lars
And I am happy with my life.

Lars Manteuffel (10)
Tweedmouth Community Middle School, Spittal

This Is Me

This is me
I like dogs
I love frogs
And monkeys too

I like games
Like Pokémon
And hate cornflakes - boo

I like quiet and peace
Because no sound is heard
Plus my favourite
SpongeBob character is Squidward

I like building things
Then rebuilding
So many things to do

And now I've grew
So this is me.

John Mcenaney (10)
Tweedmouth Community Middle School, Spittal

Just Me

My name is Alice
I live in a palace

I am funny like a buzzy bee
That's just me

I am funny
Like a cheeky bunny

I am silly
But I don't like chilli

I am shy
And I love the blue sky

I am annoying
But I don't enjoy it

I am as quiet as a mouse
And I have a big house

This is just me.

Alice Brown (10)
Tweedmouth Community Middle School, Spittal

This Is Me!

I am good at basketball, shooting hoops
I can't stand any flavours of soup
Tigers and lions are my favourite beasts
I like hot places just like Spain
I will thank you for a pizza feast
I am as amusing as a comedian
And you can thank me for a laugh
I am sporty but not arty
I am a Liverpool fan but never an Everton fan
I am a rugby fan but never a geographer.

Aidan Johnstone (11)
Tweedmouth Community Middle School, Spittal

This Is Me!

I am as quiet as a mouse
I can be sweet and salty
Nothing in this world will ever stop me
I'm scared of roller coasters and big rides
If you see how scared I get, you will be surprised
Ruby, Ruby, Ruby, that's my name
I can't change myself, I'm me, me, me
I love to cook, I love reading books
Even without a crown, I'm a queen, queen, queen.

Ruby Lambert (10)
Tweedmouth Community Middle School, Spittal

This Is Me

I am like water, I can be cold, warm and hot, but
A lso salty and
M ostly I am sparkly

Y oga isn't for me
A pples are too sweet
S and is too soft for me
M aybe I'm just a freak?
E ggs are just a no for me
E lves are too scary, but most importantly
N o one will ever be me.

Yasmeen Eldessouky (10)
Tweedmouth Community Middle School, Spittal

This Is Me

I am nice and kind
I have a nice mind
I like Spider-Man
I try as hard as I can

I like to draw
I find crystals from the core
I also like stones from the shore
I like to walk and swim
I'm like a dolphin with a fin

I like to cook cakes
But I can be a real bake
I'd like to own a zoo
With elephants and a kangaroo.

Camila Martins (10)
Tweedmouth Community Middle School, Spittal

All About Me

My eyes are as blue as the sky
My hair is as blonde as the beach
I am as silly as a monkey
I am as happy as a hippo
And as fast as a fox

My head does the hard work
But my legs are what win the race
My feet kicks the ball
Score! Back of the net!
That's just me, me, me

Plus being creative
This is just me, me, me.

Theo Forrest (10)
Tweedmouth Community Middle School, Spittal

Me

I'm as nice as a slug
I play FIFA because I like it
I play football because I'm good at it
My cat is black and white, like Postman Pat's
I eat food because it's yummy
I have big eyes that watch telly
I have thick, black hair because
I haven't had a haircut
I have a smiley face because I'm happy
That's me!

Dexter Hogarth-Johnson (11)
Tweedmouth Community Middle School, Spittal

This Is Me

Every Sunday I wake up
Ready for the day ahead
Then I look outside, wow
It's such a beautiful day
I notice it's 9:30
How am I this lazy?
Wait! Rugby is in an hour
So I better get a shower

I eat my cereal
Perfect timing, my grandad is here too
Take me to rugby
Which is my favourite sport
So I play well.

Rhys Morrison (10)
Tweedmouth Community Middle School, Spittal

Me!

I am as historical as King Tut
And don't say but...

I love beetles, especially the band
I am as scientific as Brian Cox
And don't tell me not.

I am as architectural as Norman Foster
I am as imaginative as 1,000 books
I am as slow as a snail on a whale
And always pale

So what can I say?
This is me!

Blake Scott (10)
Tweedmouth Community Middle School, Spittal

All About Me

I like to play football all day
McDonald's is my favourite takeaway
I love to ride my bike
But I hate to hike

I love my cat
Although it is really fat
My favourite food is pizza
My hands are as cold as a freezer

I jump as high as a frog
And I have one dog
I like my family
This poem is all about me.

Mason Mitchell (11)
Tweedmouth Community Middle School, Spittal

All About Me

I'm as loud as a hungry cat
As silly as a monkey
I'm as tall as a giraffe
As annoying as a squealing bat

I'm as smart as a chimpanzee
As friendly as a capybara
As sneaky as a mouse
As weird as someone causing drama

Well, that's the end
Hope you enjoyed
This little poem
All about me.

Ryan Young (10)
Tweedmouth Community Middle School, Spittal

This Is Me

I am very artistic
While my drawings are realistic
I have a lot of technique
And I am very unique
I have my flaws
And my dogs have paws
I live on the coast
Where my dog's name is Ghos
One of my brothers is a baby
And my other dog's name is Sadie
I've never been stung by a bee
But I am proud to be me!

Chloe Renner (11)
Tweedmouth Community Middle School, Spittal

I Am As...

I am as mad as a scientist
I am as sad as a cloud on a rainy day
I am as happy as the sun
I am as Irish as an Irish potato
I am as bouncy as a basketball, if I'm good I go where I need to be
I am as naughty as a puppy
I am as nervous as a fox
I am like a car, if I'm tired I won't start
This is me.

Jack Wardhaugh (11)
Tweedmouth Community Middle School, Spittal

My Hamster The Gangster

Me and Kayla
We eat dinner
We love eating veggies
Although she does love wormies
Well... 'cause she's a hamster
And a very cute gangster!

Once she bit me
But then was sorry
It's okay because I never worried!
That's okay, it's my pet!
But she will never bite you, I bet!

Layla Brown (11)
Tweedmouth Community Middle School, Spittal

This Is Me

This is me, this is me
I love sports like an athlete especially football
I love colours all of them like a rainbow
My pets keep me going like food and water
Food, of course, it keeps me alive
School is fun when all my friends are there
Friends and family are the best!
This is me, this is me.

Maisie Wright (11)
Tweedmouth Community Middle School, Spittal

This Is Me

I am not very good at darts
Especially once the opponent starts
I get so excited when I hit 180
Haha! I beat you every time matey

Bullseye, bullseye, double tops
Hopefully, my snakebite darts don't drop
My snakebite darts are very cool
Hopefully, they don't fall in the pool.

Shaun Murray
Tweedmouth Community Middle School, Spittal

This Is Me

I am as arty as a paintbrush
I am as clean as a doctor
I am as bright as a light bulb
I am as loud as a speaker
My hair is brown like chocolate
I am as colourful as a paint pallet
And of course
I am as hungry as a monster
And I am as cheeky as a monkey

This is me!

Ruby Buchan (11)
Tweedmouth Community Middle School, Spittal

How To Make Me

In a big bowl, mix 200 grams of happiness
With a pinch of morning grumpiness
Add two shimmering hazel eyes
Add smiling lips that laugh with surprise
And some hair, as brown as a bear
That sparkles in the sky
And stir in the loudness of a lion

And there you have... me!

Robyn Mason (11)
Tweedmouth Community Middle School, Spittal

All About Me

I am a wild hunter
I act like an eel
I encountered a Spheal
I love eating pizza
With a bit of pepperoni

I love sports, my favourite is football
Followed by basketball
I am as shy as a fish
I love Milky Bar mousse
I have nothing else to say
This is me.

James Gibson (10)
Tweedmouth Community Middle School, Spittal

This Is Me

One day I was looking at a toucan,
While I was holding an action figure of Venom,
While my mum was wearing denim,
I also like carrots, I'm a bit like a parrot!
I quite like bears, especially when they scare!
I love my family, I love their personalities,
I love being me.

Noel Howe (10)
Tweedmouth Community Middle School, Spittal

All About Me

I am as quiet as a mouse
I am as funny as a comedian
I am as kind as a nurse
I am as caring as a parent
I am as good-eyed as an eagle
I am as smart as a dolphin
I am as talented as a seal
I am as arty as a paintbrush
I am as messy as mud
This is me!

Jack Hoskins (10)
Tweedmouth Community Middle School, Spittal

The Ways That I Am All Day

I'm as crazy as a cat
As funny as a fox
As sporty as a cheetah
But sometimes likes to be as lonely as an empty box

I like music like Mozart
And I'm as smart as Einstein
I am as loud as the drums
But can be as quiet as the chimes.

Mason Graham (11)
Tweedmouth Community Middle School, Spittal

This Is Me!

I like dogs and football
But gaming is the best
I'm a fierce tiger
Ready to pounce
Like a beach ball bounces

I am a fierce tiger for a reason
I have a bad temper
But I'm also cheerful
Like a chipmunk
My team is Newcastle.

Taylor Burgon (11)
Tweedmouth Community Middle School, Spittal

This Is Me!

I am...
Into art
As helpful as a nurse
As daring as an adventurer
Into sloths
As picky as a cat
As messy as a dolphin
Into cats and my favourite is called Honey
Into giving
As polite as a queen
As shy as a mouse
Into gaming.

Isabelle Turley (11)
Tweedmouth Community Middle School, Spittal

This Is Me

I am as fast as lightning
As sporty as an athlete
I love going fishing with my dad catching mackerel
I also love fruit
But I also like chocolate
I am a crazy football fan
I am a class right back
I am as funny as a comedian
This is me!

Toby Trotter (10)
Tweedmouth Community Middle School, Spittal

Just Me

I am as funny as a monkey
I am as kind as a panda
I can jump as high as a frog
And have a brain that tries hard at maths

I love to play cricket
I am as smart as Einstein
I love to play with my friends
This is just me, me, me.

Mackenzie Purvis (10)
Tweedmouth Community Middle School, Spittal

This Is Me!

I'm generous and funny
I'm as soft as a bunny

A super-creative mind
Where history is my favourite
But maths makes me crazy!

I'm passionate and yellow
I like marshmallows
And I'm as quiet as a mouse.

Trulli Hogg (10)
Tweedmouth Community Middle School, Spittal

This Is Me

I like apples and dogs
I also like to read catalogues
I listen to music and YouTube
I like to solve a Rubix cube
I like to play sports like rugby
I can be a little clumsy
I like to play Xbox
I've got some cool tops.

Luis Palmero-Iglesias (11)
Tweedmouth Community Middle School, Spittal

This Is Me

I like cats and dogs
I also like doing jobs
I really like doing art
I never tear it apart

I really like playing Roblox
I also love a fox
I stay up at night
To see the sky
I love to play with fidgets.

Laila-May Blackie (10)
Tweedmouth Community Middle School, Spittal

This Is Me

I am a rugby player
I also like F1
It is fun
I like Paul Walker
I've also bought clothes from Footlocker
I am also a sleepwalker

I am also a gamer
I like to play games
I also have an Xbox name.

Dylan Flatman (10)
Tweedmouth Community Middle School, Spittal

This Is Me

I have flamy orange hair
I am as bossy
As a cat is angry

My family are generous
So am I
My friends are nice
So am I

I am tall as my mum
And most of my friends

This is me.

Leon Powling (11)
Tweedmouth Community Middle School, Spittal

This Is Me

I am a golden golfer
My favourite month is December

I love winter
I also love summer

I am not a good fighter
I like to think I'm bright and I like night

This is me!

Harry Curle (10)
Tweedmouth Community Middle School, Spittal

This Is Me

I am generous and funny
I am as silly as a kitten
I am as funny as a comedian
I am as friendly as a puppy
I am as smart as a scientist
I am as lazy as a sloth
I am as helpful as a nurse.

Finley Bartell (11)
Tweedmouth Community Middle School, Spittal

Me

I'm as fast as a fox
But as lazy as a log
I'm as loud as the sea
But as shy as a bee
I'm as boring as a worm
But as annoying as a wasp

This is me!

Savannah Brown (10)
Tweedmouth Community Middle School, Spittal

My Favourite Animal

I love dogs
Fat or skinny
Soft or fluffy
I don't mind

Small or tall
Playful or boring
I don't mind

They will always be the best of all.

Lilly Tait (10)
Tweedmouth Community Middle School, Spittal

This Is Me

There is only one of me
I am always as busy as a bee
I love dogs and cats
I also have a pet rat
I like basketball
I am also very tall.

Jake Fleming (11)
Tweedmouth Community Middle School, Spittal

This Is Me

I am strong
I am kind
And I can draw like a butterfly

Alyssa is my name
I like to play games
Blockman Go and Fortnite.

Alyssa Tucker (10)
Tweedmouth Community Middle School, Spittal

This Is Me

I am fun
I am sweet
I am sour
Depending on the hour
I am as funny as a comedian
And as lazy as a sloth.

Alexia Catterall (11)
Tweedmouth Community Middle School, Spittal

YoungWriters Est. 1991

YOUNG WRITERS INFORMATION

We hope you have enjoyed reading this book – and that you will continue to in the coming years.

If you're the parent or family member of an enthusiastic poet or story writer, do visit our website **www.youngwriters.co.uk/subscribe** and sign up to receive news, competitions, writing challenges and tips, activities and much, much more! There's lots to keep budding writers motivated!

If you would like to order further copies of this book, or any of our other titles, then please give us a call or order via your online account.

Young Writers
Remus House
Coltsfoot Drive
Peterborough
PE2 9BF
(01733) 890066
info@youngwriters.co.uk

Join in the conversation!
Tips, news, giveaways and much more!

YoungWritersUK **YoungWritersCW** **youngwriterscw**